THE LION KING

AF074100

The sun was rising over the African plain, and the animals and birds were standing together by Pride Rock.

"There he is!" one of them shouted suddenly. "There's the new prince!"

"Welcome, Prince Simba!" everyone cheered, stamping their feet on the ground.

Everyone was quiet as they watched Rafiki, a wise old baboon, raise the lion cub high into the air.

The clouds disappeared and the sun shone. Rafiki gave Simba back to his proud parents, King Mufasa and Queen Sarabi.

What a special day!

Little Simba had lots to learn. One morning, Mufasa the king took his son for a walk around the kingdom.
"Remember," said Mufasa. "A good king must respect all creatures. We are all part of the Circle of Life."

Later that day, Simba saw his uncle, Scar. Simba told Scar that he had seen the whole kingdom.

"Everywhere?" Scar asked, slyly. "Even the far north?"

"Well, no," replied Simba sadly. His father had told him not to go that far.

"Quite right," said Scar. "Only brave lions can go there. A young prince should not go to the elephant graveyard."

Simba hurried to find his best friend, a young lioness called Nala.

Simba and Nala decided to go to the elephant graveyard that day, even though they had been told to keep well away.

Scar quietly ordered three hyenas to go to the elephant graveyard too. Scar wanted them to kill Simba so that he could become king of Mufasa's kingdom.

Simba and Nala ran across the dry land to the elephant graveyard. At last, they reached a pile of bones. They had arrived.
"I don't like this place," said Nala. "Where are we?"

"This is the elephant graveyard," Simba cried as he saw a skull. Then he saw Zazu, his father's friend.

"You must leave straight away!" said Zazu. "It's dangerous!"

But it was too late! They were trapped. Three hyenas surrounded them. They were laughing nastily and licking their lips hungrily.

Simba tried to roar, but he could only make a small, squeaky sound. The hyenas laughed hysterically. Simba tried to roar again.

ROAAAARRRR! The three hyenas turned around and saw ... King Mufasa!

The king hit them with his huge paws. The hyenas ran away screaming.

Nala and Zazu went on ahead, and Mufasa walked home slowly with Simba.

"Simba, I'm disappointed. You didn't listen to me, and you put yourself and others in great danger."

Simba felt terrible. "I wanted to be brave like you," he explained.

"You don't need to go looking for trouble to prove that you're brave," said the king kindly.

The moon was shining brightly, and the stars twinkled in the dark sky.

"Look at the stars!" said Mufasa. "The great kings of the past are looking down on us. Remember that they will always be there to guide you. And so will I."

"I'll remember," replied Simba.

Scar thought of another plan to get rid of Mufasa and Simba.

He took Simba to the bottom of a gorge and told him to wait for his father. Then, the hyenas started a stampede through the herd of wildebeest.

Mufasa was walking along the rocks with Zasu. "Simba, I'm coming!" he called.

Mufasa ran to rescue his son.

But as he ran, Mufasa fell over the cliff. He saw his brother look down at him.

"Help me, Scar!" cried Mufasa. But Scar leant towards him and whispered, "Long live the king!"

Then, he pushed Mufasa in front of the wildebeest.

Simba ran to Mufasa. "Father," Simba cried. But the king did not reply. Simba started sobbing.

"This is your fault, Simba," lied Scar. "What have you done? The king has died. Don't go near the other lions ever again. Run away and don't come back."

Scar went back to Pride Rock to be crowned king. Simba dragged himself through the dry land towards the jungle. He was scared and trembling. He fell to the floor, exhausted. Large, hungry birds flew above him.

At last, Simba opened his eyes. A warthog called Pumbaa, and a meerkat called Timon were staring down at him. They gave him water to drink.

"You nearly died," said Pumbaa. "We saved you."

"Thank you for your help," replied Simba. "But it doesn't matter. I have nowhere to go."

"Why don't you stay with us?" asked Timon kindly. "Forget about the past, and don't worry."

Simba thought for a moment before deciding to stay in the jungle with his new friends.

Many years later, Simba rescued Pumbaa from being eaten by a hungry lioness. It was Nala! The two friends were very happy to see each other again.

Nala told Simba that Scar was a very mean king.

"Will you come back to Pride Rock, Simba?" asked Nala. "You should be king!"

But Simba was worried that he didn't deserve to be king.

Simba showed Nala his favourite places in the jungle.
"It's beautiful here," said Nala. "But it's not your home."
She turned and left her friend on his own.

That night, Simba lay by a stream, thinking. Suddenly, he heard a sound. He looked up and saw Rafiki. Rafiki had travelled far to find Simba.

"Come with me," said Rafiki. "I can take you to your father."

Simba followed Rafiki to the stream.

Simba looked at his reflection in the water. The reflection was changing, and suddenly, he saw his father's face.

Simba heard Mufasa's voice: "Simba. You must take your place in the Circle of Life. You are my son, the true king."
Then the reflection, and Rafiki, disappeared.

Back at Pride Rock, it had not rained for a long time and the land was dry.

"We're hungry!" moaned the hyenas to King Scar. "There's no food here for us."

There were black, stormy clouds in the sky and lightning struck the earth. The dry grass around Pride Rock caught fire. A large lion came out of the smoke and flames. It was Simba!

Scar lunged at Simba. He wanted to kill him like he had killed Mufasa. The two fought fiercely. Simba pushed Scar over the cliff. Simba had won!

Nala went to Simba's side. "Welcome home!" she whispered. The two smiled at each other. Then, it started raining.

Heavy raindrops fell on the wet earth. Before long, the streams were full of water once more. Things began to grow on the land, and the animals came back.

Early one morning, the animals and birds went to Pride Rock once again.

Everyone watched as Rafiki picked up a young cub in his hands.

Everyone celebrated as they saw a new princess.

This was the daughter of King Simba and Queen Nala.

That night, Simba looked at the stars shining in the sky.

"Everything's all right, Father," said Simba, quietly. "I remembered."

And the stars twinkled back at him.